"From the pe  evangelist and c the Gospel comes this concise anu c. tion of the true Gospel. Mark Ballard succinctly dispels with a host of attempts to saddle the Gospel of salvation with non-salvific encumberments of social reform. He graciously exposes the fallacy of the fashionable elevating of social concerns to 'Gospel issues,' which transforms the simple Gospel into a complex message of opinions, thereby obscuring the true Gospel.

Mark masterfully and precisely distinguishes between the essentials of the Gospel and results from the Gospel. Mark's cogent and precise style reasserts the uniqueness and priority of the Gospel of salvation. This book is undoubtedly an essential read for the scholar, student, and everyone who desires clarity about the Gospel so people can hear God's astonishing message of salvation."

- **Ronnie Rogers**
Pastor, Trinity Baptist Church
Norman, Oklahoma

"When I was a teenager, I worked for a man who would say, 'Ain't that the gospel!' in response to anything he agreed with or felt good about. For him, 'Gospel' was simply a positive term with no clear referent or meaning. Sadly a similar thing can be said about the way some in the church use the term 'Gospel' today. What does it mean to 'preach the Gospel,' or to be a 'Gospel-centered' ministry? What is a 'Gospel issue'? Too often, the word 'Gospel' becomes a plastic-elastic entity in our usage, and the word is either emptied of part of its scriptural significance or infused with a meaning we have created for it. Instead, the Gospel – the saving truth of Jesus' atoning death and resurrection – is a real, unalterable, life-transforming, supernatural message. Dr. Mark Ballard's latest book, *Words Matter: What Is the Gospel?* provides a clear biblical perspective on the meaning of the Gospel, and offers real-world guidance for how to share the Gospel with others."

- **Stephen Rummage**
Senior Pastor, Quail Springs Baptist Church
Oklahoma City, Oklahoma

"Spiritual leaders tend to attach the word 'Gospel' to many of their social causes. While their goal may be worthwhile, it often confuses people about the Biblical message of salvation. In *Words Matter: What Is the Gospel?*, Dr. Mark Ballard presents a clear understanding of the Gospel and reminds us of the danger of using the word 'Gospel' in a careless way. His words will challenge and convict any person who teaches or preaches God's Word."

- **Phil Waldrep**
President, Phil Waldrep Ministries
Decatur, Alabama

"Mark Ballard has done an incredible job emphasizing the critical need to understand the nature of the Gospel. The Gospel is not complicated . . . Christ died for our sins, was buried and raised from the dead. It is all about salvation. The Gospel is that simple. Our lives will be transformed when we are saved, but don't confuse the results of the Gospel with the Gospel itself. The Gospel is the offer of grace from a loving God. It is for us to receive by faith."

- **Jimmy Draper**
President Emeritus, Lifeway
Colleyville, TX

WORDS MATTER

Words Matter

What Is the Gospel?

MARK H. BALLARD

Timothy K. Christian

Northeastern Baptist Press

Words Matter
What Is the Gospel?
Copyright © 2020 by Mark H. Ballard & Timothy K. Christian

Published by Northeastern Baptist Press
             Post Office Box 4600
             Bennington, VT 05201

Cover design by Leason "Tripper" Stiles III

Paperback ISBN: 978-1-953331-00-7
ePub ISBN: 978-1-953331-01-4

To our children,

Benjamin Enoch Zhijiang Ballard
Trina Maria Silva & Timothy Marcus Christian

CONTENTS

INTRODUCTION

Several years ago I pastored in Deerfield, Virginia. One Sunday, after the evening service, a church member asked, "Can I visit you at the parsonage next Tuesday?"

"Sure," I said. "Would you like to set a specific time?"

"Will you be home in the evening?"

"Yes. We plan to go to Staunton that day, but we should be home all evening. What time works for you?"

"Well, I'm not sure of an exact time," he said. "I'll be over sometime in the evening."

We made our trip to Staunton on Tuesday and were careful to be home by 3:00 in the afternoon. We completed some projects, prepared for our guest, had dinner, and waited ... and waited. But he didn't come.

The next evening, as I prepared the worship-center for our mid-week service, the man entered the building and walked directly to me. With apparent agitation he said, "Preacher, you lied to me!"

I greeted him by name and asked, "What do you mean?"

He said, "I went to see you Tuesday evening, but you weren't home."

"I'm confused," I said. "We were home all evening. In fact, we waited for you until 10:00. We expected you. We were watching and listening for you."

"There you go lying again! I came to your house. I knocked on the door. I even went around and knocked on the back door. No one was there."

"I don't know how we could have missed you."

"You're lying to me again! Your car wasn't even in the driveway."

At that moment I suspected the problem. It seemed we were using the same vocabulary, but a different dictionary.

"Wait a minute," I said. "Did you come Tuesday evening?"

"Yes!"

"What does 'evening' mean to you?"

He said, "Anytime after lunch and before 4:00 PM."

"What time did you come to our house?"

"Around 2:00."

"Now we've discovered the problem," I said. "We got home around 3:00 PM."

"But you said you'd be home all evening."

"Yes," I said. "Where I grew up, evening meant after 6:00 PM and before 9:00 PM."

WORDS AND DEFINITIONS

Words are important; so are definitions. If we use the same words but different meanings we don't communicate. We confuse.

If this is true in general conversation, it's especially true when we study and teach the Bible. Correct, clear, and consistent use of biblical words and their definitions is vital. Why? The Bible deals with God's revelation and our eternal destinies.

WHAT IS THE GOSPEL?

For example, the Bible commands everyone to believe the Gospel.[1] Simple enough. Yet, to obey the command we must correctly define the Gospel. We must know what we are commanded to believe.

The Greek word translated "Gospel" is *euangelíon*. It is a compound word. It combines *eú*, meaning good or well, and *angéllō*, meaning to proclaim or tell.[2] The Gospel means to tell, declare, or proclaim good news.

The "Gospel" is not generic good news. It is a specific kind of good news. If your doctor says, "It's not cancer," if your child says, "I love you," if the Director of the Homeless Shelter says, "You provided 900 meals for our clients this year," it is good news. But it is not the Biblical Gospel.

In the New Testament, the Gospel refers "only to the glad tidings of Christ and His salvation."[3] It is the good news of how Jesus Christ conquers our sins and gives eternal life to all who believe in Him.

THE GOSPEL CAN BE CONFUSED

If, however, we use a different dictionary and re-define the Gospel, the confusion will be far more serious than dropping by to visit a friend who isn't home. Confusion about the true meaning of the Gospel will result in people missing heaven and landing in hell.

THE GOSPEL CAN BE MISUSED

"The Gospel" is the narrow focus of this book. The present day misuse of the word among evangelicals, including among my fellow Baptists, concerns me. Is the misuse unintentional? Perhaps. For some. Is it subtle? Certainly. Is it confusing? Definitely. Does it matter? Absolutely. Allow me to explain.

The Bible clearly defines the Gospel—the good news we believe and proclaim. It includes three indispensible truths.[4]

1. Jesus Christ's substitutionary death for sinners—"Christ died for our sins."
2. Jesus Christ's necessary burial—He was actually dead; He did not just appear dead.

3. Jesus Christ's physical resurrection—"He rose again the third day."

To be born again a sinner, separated from God, must believe these simple facts. They are non-negotiable. These three simple facts lead us to singular faith in a qualified Savior. The three facts declare what Jesus Christ, God in the flesh, did for us. He was punished in our place so that we can go free. We turn from our sin and self and trust Jesus Christ alone for our salvation.

These facts are simple enough for a child to understand, believe, and be saved. They are clear enough to humble an intellectual, leading him or her to trust Jesus Christ with thankful child-like faith. What is my concern?

MUCH ADO ABOUT SOMETHING

Speakers and writers often load "the Gospel" with excess baggage. They connect the Gospel to multiple items and issues that have little or no relationship to the biblical Gospel.

Perhaps you have heard some or all of the following statements.

- "Believers should live Gospel-centered lives."
- "It's all about the Gospel."

- "It's the Gospel truth."
- "Plan for Gospel conversations."

The statements may or may not be valid. It depends on ones definition of the Gospel. And that is my point. Words matter.

"Gospel" is applied to an array of issues. For example, "It's a Gospel issue," is a popular all-encompassing phrase in evangelical circles. I have heard "Gospel issue" related to:

- Race relations
- Social work
- Social justice
- Immigration
- Abortion
- Adoption
- Women's rights
- Identity politics
- Critical Race Theory
- Intersectionality
- Religious Liberty

This list, I assure you, is only partial.

A Gospel Issue

First, "What is a 'Gospel issue'?" What does the term mean?

One blogger formulated a definition based on its

general use in multiple articles. "A 'Gospel issue,'" he stated, "is one that is essential to a right understanding and practice of the Christian life for those who believe the Gospel."[5] However, he also noted, "It seems that the expression 'Gospel issue' is a rhetorical move to lend urgency, moral, and spiritual significance to a given point of view."[6]

Some ask, "What's the problem? What's wrong with making a genuine concern more urgent and significant? Besides, what's wrong with a social issue being connected to a Gospel believer's 'right understanding and practice of the Christian life'? How does that confuse the Gospel? How does it misuse the Gospel? Aren't you being a bit hypercritical? How does the term 'Gospel issue' redefine the Gospel?"

Those are important questions. They deserve a clear answer.

When Jesus Christ's Gospel transforms us, He impacts every area of our lives. However, believing 'the Gospel' for salvation is distinct from sanctification—growing in the Christian life. If one speaks of an action as if it were an essential tenet of the Gospel, one redefines the Gospel. That's true no matter how good or valid the activity may be. Law is not grace.

Feeding the poor is good, but it is not an essential Gospel tenet. Defending the unborn is vital, but it is not the Gospel. Religious Liberty is a Baptist distinctive, but it is not the Gospel. Voting for or against a specific candidate is not the Gospel. Social justice is not the Gospel. Caring for widows and orphans is a mark of "pure and undefiled religion,"[7] but it is not the Gospel.

Believers can love the Lord our God with all our hearts, souls, and minds. We can love our neighbors as ourselves. According to Jesus, these are the first and second greatest commandments.[8] Perhaps leaders who identify multiple social issues as "Gospel issues" intend to urge believers to obey the second greatest commandment. If so, I agree with the sentiment but it makes my point. It confuses and misuses the Gospel.

An example will help. Phil Johnson is the Executive Director of "Grace To You"—John MacArthur's radio, TV, and internet program. A woman confronted him following a morning worship service. She wanted to help Phil understand "the 'social justice' issue."[9]

> "Despite what you think," she said, "it is a Gospel issue. Injustice is everywhere in the world. I am fighting it full time. Right now I have several lawsuits pending against injustice in the health-care industry. Don't tell me that's not Gospel work. You're not being a faithful witness unless you're fighting for social justice. It's built right into the Gospel message: 'You shall love your neighbor as yourself.'"[10]

The woman was sincere and zealous. But she had been led astray. She had confused the "second great commandment" with the Gospel.

Phil tried to encourage as well as clarify. Their conversation continued.

> "That's surely one of the most important tenets of God's moral law, and it *does* distill the idea of human justice into a single commandment," [Johnson] said. "But be careful how you state it. That's not the *Gospel*. That's the Second Great Commandment."
>
> "Oh, right," she said. "I meant to say the Gospel is 'You shall love the Lord your God with all your heart, soul, and mind.'"
>
> "Well, that's the *First* Great Commandment," [he] said. "That's still law, not Gospel." ...
>
> "But it's in the Bible," she repeated. "So it's a Gospel issue."[11]

And so the confusion grows. The law cannot save. That was never its purpose. The law convicts of sin and the need for a Savior. The law reprimands; it multiples guilt.[12] Then it takes us by the hand and leads us to Jesus.[13] No amount of good works or law keeping can make one right with God.[14]

"Love the LORD your God"[15] is not the biblical Gospel. It is a result of the Gospel, but it is not the Gospel. "Love your neighbor as yourself"[16] will not break sin's chains. Neighborly love cannot make one a child of God. Such a "Gospel conversation" is a false, social Gospel conversation. Johnson observed:

Blending the Gospel with social activism has been tried many times. (Google "Walter Rauschenbusch" or "social Gospel.") It has always turned out to be a shortcut to Socinianism,[17] carnal humanism,[18] or some more sinister form of spiritual barrenness. The social message inevitably overwhelms and *replaces* the Gospel message, no matter how well intentioned proponents of the method may have been at the start.[19]

"To insist that social justice activism is an essential tenet of Gospel truth is a form of theological legalism."[20] The same can be said for any other activity. Paul warned the Galatians against adding law to the Gospel. The crusaders in Galatia tried to make Jewish dietary laws and circumcision essential Gospel tenets.[21] Paul would have none of it. He said,

[6] I marvel that you are turning away so soon from Him who called you in the grace of Christ, to a different [kind of[22]] Gospel, [7] which is not another [of the same kind[23]]; but there are some who trouble you and want to pervert the Gospel of Christ. [8] But even if we, or an angel from heaven, preach any other Gospel to you than what we have preached to you, let him be accursed. [9] As we have said before, so now I say again, if anyone preaches any other Gospel to you than what you have received, let him be accursed.[24]

Paul accepted no additions to the Gospel. Additions do not purify the Gospel; they "pervert" it. He warned, "A little leaven leavens the whole lump."[25] Adding to the Gospel leads to the proverbial "slippery-slope." Loosely referring to anything and everything as a "Gospel issue" robs the Biblical Gospel of its meaning and power. *That which means everything ultimately means nothing.*

When evangelical leaders use "Gospel" as a nebulous catchall term, their followers are defenseless when non-evangelicals appropriate the term. A recent example made the national news.

A non-evangelical minister condemned Bible-believing conservative Christians who speak against "same sex marriage" and unique "LGBTQ+ rights." Authoritatively he declared, "Frankly, they are denying the Gospel of Jesus Christ."

When trusted evangelical leaders repeatedly declare that women's rights, social justice, identity politics, etc., are "Gospel issues," how will their disciples respond to such a statement? Will they question their previous resistance to the movement for LGBTQ+ normalization? Will they question a literal interpretation of the Bible? After all, no genuine Christian wants to be guilty of "denying the Gospel of Jesus Christ."

Words matter; so do their definitions. When a word is isolated from its definition, loaded with excess baggage and used broadly, it looses its meaning and significance. In contrast, the Biblical Gospel is not a broad nebulous term. The Gospel is **CRUCIAL**,

CLEAR, CERTAIN, and **SERIOUS.** To these we now turn.

1

The Gospel Is

CRUCIAL

The Apostle Paul declared the Gospel's cruciality to his friends in Corinth. His urgency was evident. He wrote, "Moreover, brethren, I declare to you the gospel which I preached to you, which also you received and in which you stand, by which also you are saved, if you hold fast that word which I preached to you—unless you believed in vain."[26]

For Paul, the Gospel was not a casual conversation. Notice:

- *How he communicated*—"I declare ... I preached ... I preached"
- *What he communicated*—"the Gospel"
- *The result of his communication*—"you received ... you stand ... you are saved"

The Gospel is crucial. It stirred Paul's heart. It stimulated his emotions and spurred him into action.

Present Message

When the church in Corinth heard Paul's letter read publicly, they received his present message. "I declare, I make the Gospel known to you right now." In that sense, the Gospel continues to be a present message. The Gospel message now goes out through God's faithful churches around the world. Churches, of course, are people rather than buildings. God's people share the Gospel personally[27] as they have conversations in day-to-day life, and corporately as they gather in local congregations for weekly praise and preaching.[28]

Past Message

Paul also noted that he "preached"—past tense—the Gospel to them.[29] It was his past message. He had not changed his message since his last visit.

Persistent Message

Further, he urged them to "hold fast that word which I preached to you."[30] Cling to it. Hold it firmly. Don't let it go. The Gospel was Paul's persistent and consistent message.

The Gospel does not evolve with the times. We are not to adjust and redefine it. Our declaration of the Gospel must be consistent. The Corinthian church then and our churches now must retain the consistent Gospel message. We "hold fast" to the Gospel. We retain it.[31] We protect its message like soldiers defending a fortress under assault.

Do you read the labels on food packages or in your medicine cabinet? For example, are you familiar with PEG-8 Dimethicone, Sodium Caproamphopropionate, or Ethylparaben? No? Neither was I. But I just wiped my hands with them before I wrote this paragraph. They are three of the sixteen ingredients in an individually packaged antibacterial hand wipe. By the way, you'll be encouraged to know it also contained Benzethonium Chloride along with the always popular PEG-60 Lanolin.

Many items on ingredient lists are hard to pronounce, much less understand. Not so with the Gospel. The contents are easy to understand. They are also essential. The Gospel's content is not mysterious or debatable. Believers must hold fast to and declare the true Gospel.

Priority Message

The Gospel was also Paul's priority message. He proclaimed the Gospel above all else. He said, "For I delivered to you first of all"[32] meaning "'of first importance.' The Gospel is the most important message that the church ever proclaims. While it is good to be involved in social action and the betterment of mankind, there is no reason why these ministries should preempt the Gospel."[33] Nor is there reason to use social action to redefine the Gospel. In fact, we must not do so.

GOSPEL PROCLAIMED

The Gospel was Paul's *past, present, persistent,* and *priority* message. The narrative of his ministry in Acts and the doctrinal instructions in all of his epistles reveals his pattern. Paul proclaimed the same Gospel wherever he went and to whomever he spoke. His message did not shift from one class or culture to another. Whether answering a prison guard's questions in Philippi,[34] reasoning with philosophers in Athens,[35] or testifying before the Jewish Council in Jerusalem,[36] his core message was the same. "Christ died for our sins, ... He was buried, and ... He rose again the third day."

The consistent content of Paul's preaching reveals his unwavering conviction—the Gospel is crucial. Everyone needs to hear it.

GOSPEL RECEIVED

Paul proclaimed the Gospel. The Corinthians "received" the Gospel. They "took it in";[37] they accepted and internalized the crucial Gospel message.

The Corinthians believed Jesus Christ died on the cross for their sins, was buried, and rose from the dead. They believed the Gospel message and responded in faith. They trusted the living Lord Jesus Christ alone for their salvation. Because they received the Gospel, Jesus Christ rescued them from their sins.

Why did they need to be rescued? Like you and me, the Corinthians were sinners. "For all have sinned and fall short of the glory of God."[38] No one meets the Father's perfect standard of righteousness. Jesus said, "Therefore you shall be perfect, just as your Father in heaven is perfect."[39]

Sin has consequences. The holy, righteous, and just Judge of the universe declared the wages that sin earns:

- Death—physical and spiritual
- Separation from God
- His just punishment[40]

Left to our own devices we are in deep trouble. Human ingenuity, philanthropy, personal reform, or religious activity cannot rescue us from sin. They cannot create a clean heart within us or deliver us from guilt.[41] Even if we could stop sinning right now, what of our past sins? Their stain remains. We are now headed for eternal separation from God in hell. We are in trouble. Big trouble. We need a Savior, and Jesus Christ is the only sufficient Savior.

The Corinthians are an encouraging example. According to Paul, the Corinthians received the Gospel in the past and were saved in the present. How? The Gospel made the difference.

Corinth was notoriously ungodly. Paul noted the sinful actions and attitudes prevalent in the city. They were "fornicators ... idolaters ... adulterers ... homosexuals[42] ... sodomites[43] ... thieves ... covetous ... drunkards ... revilers ... [and] extortioners."[44] They were doomed.

Paul warned, "Such people will not 'inherit the kingdom of God.'"[45] No doubt about it, even if they have endured racial bigotry, social injustice, and economic oppression. However, he added some good news. "And such were some of you. But you were washed, but you were sanctified, but you were justified in the name of the Lord Jesus and by the Spirit of our God."[46] Now everything was changed. They were saved and forgiven. They enjoyed a right relationship with God. Why? They believed the Gospel and Jesus Christ transformed their lives.

The Gospel is crucial. When one hears, believes, and responds to the Gospel, he/she is saved. This crucial Gospel was Paul's primary message.

No Compromise

Because the Gospel was crucial, Paul warned the church not to compromise the message. He noted, "Since you 'stand' in the Gospel, 'hold fast' to the Gospel."[47] The simple, clear, uncompromised

Gospel—Jesus Christ's sacrificial death, necessary burial, and literal bodily resurrection—is crucial.

The same is true for you, for me, and for our churches. We can "stand firm" in the Gospel—set free from past sins. We can "hold fast" to the Gospel—no compromise. The Gospel is our priority message.

DISTRACTED MESSENGERS

Distraction is an ever-present danger. Gospel messengers must be attentive. Even those who have known the Lord and declared His Gospel for many years can be distracted from the crucial Gospel message. Social service can eclipse Gospel sharing. Calling it a "Gospel issue" won't change the reality; it won't introduce even one soul to Jesus Christ and His saving grace.

Several years ago Cindy and I moved to North Carolina for graduate work. We left a church-planting ministry in Texas so I could work on a master's degree at Southeastern Baptist Theological Seminary. I did not pastor a church the first few months we lived in Wake Forest. We joined a congregation just outside the city limits. The church was serious about proclaiming the Gospel from the pulpit on Sundays and throughout the week. Many of the church members shared the Gospel with friends, neighbors, and strangers.

On Tuesday nights several church members gathered at the building for training. After the training, teams of three visited those who had recently visited a church service or activity. A team would go to their home and get to know them. The teams answered questions about the church's ministries and beliefs. They also asked permission to share the Gospel. Cindy and I joined this exciting ministry.

Through the evangelistic ministry we met many church and community members. We often learned their stories. One church couple shared a shocking story. At least I was shocked. The couple had been international missionaries for thirty-five years. One Tuesday evening during a fellowship time they noted their excitement about sharing the Gospel. Someone commented, "I guess you really miss sharing the Gospel on the mission field."

A sad look clouded their faces. They glanced at one another before the wife spoke.

"No," she confessed, "we never shared the Gospel before we joined this ministry."

She went on to explain. "We spent our ministry lives on foreign soil. We fed the hungry. We clothed the poor. We helped the sick get medical attention. But we never shared the Gospel."

She could have added, "For thirty-five years we worked for the largest missionary organization in the world. We were missionaries in good standing. We received good reviews. Other missionaries respected us. But no one received Jesus Christ as a result of our ministry. Our good works were not Gospel conduits. Neither of us shared the Gospel with a single person.

We didn't learn how to share the Gospel until we retired from our missionary work. A church that made the Gospel a priority changed our lives. We finally learned that the Gospel is crucial."

Today, a verbal and growing number of Christians and churches have moved social needs and social justice to the forefront. They are now priority issues. I'm troubled by this growing trend, especially within my Baptist denomination. Why? The churches are headed toward the same ministry results lamented by my friends after thirty-five barren years of social missionary work.

Ministries to the underprivileged, neglected, and abused are good and biblical if they are conduits for the Gospel.[48] That only happens, however, if the Gospel is primary and social ministry is secondary.

Let me be blunt. What difference will it make if Christians give warm clothes and vitamin-enriched food, but do not present the Gospel? What eternal difference will it make if we give every oppressed group the dignity and respect they deserve, but do not give them the Gospel? What difference will it make if we proclaim that these are "Gospel issues"? Without a true, simple, clear Gospel presentation and invitation, people will be eternally separated from God in hell.

UNDISTRACTED MESSENGERS

Bible believing churches can keep the Gospel primary. Social ministry must remain secondary. It can be an effective tool for presenting the Biblical Gospel.

Paul agreed.

Undistracted by Injustice

There were massive social needs in first century Rome. Hundreds of thousands of slaves served Roman masters. The poor lived in crowded, unsanitary conditions while the rich and powerful lived lavish, self-indulgent lives. The chasm between the haves and the have-nots was a Grand Canyon.

Many in ancient Rome desperately needed justice. Injustice was blatant. One example paints the picture. Claudius, the Roman Emperor, in an act of systemic racism and bigotry, expelled all Jews from Rome.[49]

In spite of the rampant inequality and injustice in their city, Paul was not distracted when he wrote to the Romans. "*I am* ready," he said, "to preach the Gospel to you who are in Rome also. For I am not ashamed of the Gospel of Christ,"—and he explained why—"for it is the power of God to salvation for everyone who believes, for the Jew first and also for the Greek."[50]

Don't miss the simple point. For the Apostle Paul, the Gospel was the priority need for everyone. It was the primary need for the oppressor and the oppressed.

It was the priority need for the disenfranchised and marginalized. And so it is today. The Gospel is still the hope for those enduring any form of injustice.

Undistracted by Inequality

The Biblical Gospel can calm social unrest, correct inequality, and cure systemic racism. The Gospel is the great equalizer.

In the New Testament era, relationships between Jews and Gentiles were often bitter. Neither group respected the other. The attitudes spilled over into the church. Many early Jewish Christians believed a Gentile could not be saved without first converting to Judaism. The conviction became a major hindrance to Paul's missionary work and prompted the first church council in Jerusalem. They debated the question, "Must a Gentile become a Jew in order to be saved?" Their conclusion was, "No." Gentiles need not become Jews, keep the law, or submit to circumcision in order to be saved.[51]

Paul whole-heartedly entered the debate. He spoke in favor of his Gentile converts and the unrevised Gospel of grace. But through it all, he refused to be distracted. He knew the Gospel was the answer for both Jews and Gentiles. He noted that God revealed a mystery: "that the Gentiles should be fellow heirs, of the same body, and partakers of His promise in Christ through the gospel."[52] Jews can accept Gentiles as absolute equals because of the Gospel.

At the same time, Paul allowed no reverse discrimination from the Gentiles toward their Jewish brothers and sisters. He said, "Therefore remember that you, once Gentiles in the flesh ... were without Christ, being aliens from the commonwealth of Israel and strangers from the covenants of promise, having no hope and without God in the world. But now in Christ Jesus you who once were far off have been brought near by the blood of Christ."[53] The Gospel is the great unifier.

Undistracted by Enslavement

Paul wrote to his friend Philemon. He was a genuine believer, but also a slave-owner. While imprisoned in Rome, Paul met Philemon's runaway slave, Onesimus. Paul led him to Christ. Onesimus ministered to him and was a great comfort during Paul's imprisonment. He wished Onesimus could stay with him but he believed it was his duty to send him back.

The brief letter to Philemon is Paul's commendation of Onesimus, who presented the letter to Philemon when he returned. Paul has been criticized as a child of his times, a perpetrator of the multiple patriarchal abuses of his day. But the criticism misses the power of the Gospel.

Paul commended Onesimus, urging Philemon to receive him "no longer as a slave but more than a slave—a beloved brother, ... both in the flesh and in the Lord."[54] Paul's point is moving. If Philemon recognized Onesimus as a brother in Christ, he could no longer see him as property to be used. He would see him as a brother to be loved, respected, and welcomed. He would see that both he and Onesimus were sinners saved by grace, made in God's image, equal brothers in Christ. The Gospel is the great equalizer.

Paul refused to be distracted from the Gospel. It was his hope and confidence. No other innovation could heal the injustice, inequality, and enslavement of his day. The Gospel was Paul's consistent priority because **THE GOSPEL IS CRUCIAL**.

We too can share this crucial Gospel if we know the Gospel's content. Which leads to our next subject.

2

The Gospel Is

C L E A R

Paul wanted the Corinthians to understand the Gospel. We have the same desire for people in our circles of influence.

Paul explained the Gospel in simple, clear language. He never tried to "wow" people with his oratorical acumen or intellectual horsepower. He had no interest in impressing people with his voluminous vocabulary. Truth was his only concern; he wanted his hearers to know and believe the truth. This was Paul's consistent passion and pattern. He stated:

[1] And I, brethren, when I came to you, did not come with excellence of speech or of wisdom declaring to you the testimony of God. [2] For I determined not to know anything among you except Jesus Christ and Him crucified. [3] I was with you in weakness, in fear, and in much trembling. [4] And my speech and my preaching *were* not with per-

suasive words of human wisdom, but in demonstration of the Spirit and of power, [5] that your faith should not be in the wisdom of men but in the power of God.[55]

Consider Paul's clear declaration of the Gospel. It is a three-fold message. The three essential tenets are sequential—the second builds on the first; the third builds on the first and second. Each part is vital and necessary.

1. Christ died for our sins. He was punished in our place. He accepted the wages of our sin—death.[56]
2. Christ was buried because He actually died.
3. Christ rose from the dead, defeating sin, death, and the grave.[57]

Paul did not make up his message. It did not originate in a creative imagination—Paul's or anyone else's. He proclaimed the Gospel on the authority of the Scriptures. Twice he stated that his message was "according to the Scriptures." The Old Testament not only prophesied the coming of the Lord Jesus,[58] it also prophesied His death, burial, and resurrection. "The Gospel according to the Scriptures" is summarized in two verses of Isaiah 53. Isaiah prophesied the three-fold content of Paul's Gospel declaration.[59]

ACCORDING TO THE SCRIPTURES

1. **Isaiah Prophesied:** "Yet it pleased the Lord to bruise Him; He has put *Him* to grief. When You make His soul an offering for sin, ..."[60] **Paul Proclaimed:** Christ died for our sins.
2. **Isaiah Prophesied:** "And they made His grave with the wicked—but with the rich at His death."[61] **Paul Proclaimed:** Christ was buried.
3. **Isaiah Prophesied:** "When You make His soul an offering for sin,[62] He shall see *His* seed, He shall prolong *His* days."[63] **Paul Proclaimed:** Christ rose from the dead, defeating sin, death, and the grave.

We could give other examples, but this one is sufficient. The Gospel was God's revelation not Paul's innovation. Consider each of the three Gospel tenets that Paul specifically declared in 1 Corinthians 15:3-4.

CHRIST DIED FOR OUR SINS

First, Jesus Christ died on the cross for our sins. To say that Jesus died is not remarkable. So did every other person who lived in the 1st century A.D. Death is a part of life. It has been since Adam and Eve ate the forbidden fruit in the Garden of Eden.[64] The latest statistics indicate that one out of one will die. That is a sad truth of living in this fallen world. Until Jesus returns, no one will escape death.

The simple fact that the Romans crucified a 1st century Jew is also unremarkable. Jesus was one of many. He was only 1 of 3 crucified at Calvary that day.[65] But there is much more to Jesus Christ's death than a typical 1st century execution. Paul summarized and highlighted it in his definition of the Gospel. Notice three realities. They make Paul's statement of Jesus's death remarkable.

His Identity

Paul first stated Jesus Christ's death in light of His remarkable identity. He used Jesus's title rather than His name. Christ is not Jesus's last name. He was not the son of Joseph and Mary Christ. The title, "Christ," is the Greek equivalent of the Hebrew word, "Messiah"—anointed one.

Prophesies concerning the Messiah go all the way back to the Garden. Adam and Eve succumbed to the serpent's satanic temptation. They ate the forbidden fruit. As a result, God cursed the serpent and Satan. Within the curse is the first Messianic prophecy in the Bible. That which is a glorious promise for us was a curse for Satan. God said, "And I will put enmity between you and the woman, and between your seed and her Seed; He shall bruise your head, and you shall bruise His heel."[66]

"Her Seed" anticipated Jesus's *virgin birth*. Every

other birth in human history required a man to provide the seed, but not the virgin birth.[67]

Further, God predicted a *vicious battle*. The "enmity between" Satan and Jesus was inevitable. Enmity means there was deep-rooted hatred[68] on Satan's part and holy wrath on God's part. Jesus engaged and won the vicious battle on the cross.[69]

Finally, the battle will conclude with a *victorious bruising*. Jesus's heel was bruised on the cross. He died. The blow was fatal but not final. He rose from the dead. Victorious. Satan's worst attack could not defeat Him. In contrast, Jesus crushed Satan's head. Satan's doom is certain, final, and eternal.[70] The Bible's first Messianic prophecy points to Jesus as clearly as if His photograph was beside the verse in your Bible.

Our culture is casual about sin. God is not. He is holy, righteous, and just. God's nature demands that He must punish sin. Sin made death an inescapable part of life on earth. Sin causes more than physical death, however. It results in eternal death, separation from God—forever—in hell.[71] Such judgment is everyone's just wage.[72] Yet here is a majestic example of God's mercy. When the first sin was committed, God responded with grace. He promised to send the Messiah to save people from their sin.[73]

God is so serious about sin that He gave His Son to pay our sin debt. No other sacrifice is sufficient to satisfy His righteous requirements.[74]

Subsequent Old Testament books added many

Messianic prophecies. With each prophecy a clearer picture of the Messiah came into focus.

Finally the Messiah came. He lived, died, and rose. Every detail of Jesus Christ's life made His identity, in light of each fulfilled Messianic prophecy, more and more clear. Now we understand; He is fully God and fully man.[75] He became flesh and dwelt among us.[76] He was tempted just as we are. Yet because He is fully God, He resisted all temptation. He never yielded. He never sinned.[77] He is the only perfect human to ever walk the earth.

The fact that the Messiah died is remarkable. Sin brings death but Christ never sinned. There was, therefore, no personal necessity for His death; yet He died. This is a remarkable fact.

His Purpose

Second, Paul stated Jesus's death in light of its remarkable purpose. He died for a remarkable reason: "for our sins." We have already established that Christ did not deserve to die; His death was not necessary because He had not earned its wages. He was sinless. Yet He willingly received our punishment.

"The wages of sin is death."[78] Why? God created Adam, placed him in the Garden of Eden, and commanded him not to eat from a particular tree. God imposed a death sentence upon disobedience to the command.

[15] Then the Lord God took the man and put him in the garden of Eden to tend and keep it. [16] And the Lord God commanded the man, saying, "Of every tree of the garden you may freely eat; [17] but of the tree of the knowledge of good and evil you shall not eat, for in the day that you eat of it you shall surely die."[79]

Adam disobeyed. He and Eve ate the forbidden fruit,[80] and the wages for sin went into effect. Adam's spiritual death (severed relationship with God) was immediate. The process of physical death also began. Death progressed in Adam until a mere 930 years later, "Adam ... died."[81] Every subsequent member of the human race received the wages of Adam's sin. "Therefore, just as through one man sin entered the world, and death through sin, and thus death spread to all men, because all sinned."[82]

Without a redeemer, a savior, a justifier, a life-giver, the human dilemma was hopeless. And that is why Jesus came and died for us. "Christ died for our sins"—yours and mine. Since "the wages of sin is death" God would not remain just if He simply overlooked or ignored sin. Therefore, Jesus Christ took the punishment we deserve. He died in our place. He endured God's holy wrath against our sin.[83] He became our substitute. The purpose of His death is remarkable.

Old Testament Prophecy

Third, Paul stated Jesus's death in light of its remarkable prediction. Christ's death was "according to the Scriptures."Long before Jesus's birth in Bethlehem the Old Testament prophets predicted Jesus's death. The first century Jewish leaders focused on the prophesies of the Messiah's coming kingdom reign. They longed for Him to deliver them from their Roman conquerors and occupiers. They largely ignored the prophecies of His death.

As noted above, of all the prophecies of Jesus's sacrificial death for our sins, none is more profound, detailed, or contemporary than Isaiah 53. Verse 6, for example, declares:

- Our need for a Savior—"All we like sheep have gone astray."
- We are dominated by selfishness and self-will—"We have turned, every one, to his own way."
- The Father provided for our need—"And the LORD has laid on Him the iniquity of us all."

Christ came and died in our place. "The Father has sent the Son as Savior of the world."[84] He endured our punishment. Isaiah prophesied it some 800 years before Jesus came. Without Christ's substitutionary death, there is no Gospel. But that's not all.

CHRIST WAS BURIED

The Gospel states that Jesus was buried. As previously noted, Isaiah prophesied Christ's death and burial. Isaiah said He would die with the wicked but be buried "with the rich."[85] Eight hundred years later, Matthew reported that Jesus died between two criminals and was buried in a rich man's tomb.[86]

Were these coincidences or coordinated deceptions? Impossible. Multiple details were fulfilled. Precisely. It could not be a coincident. Nor could it be a coordinated deception. His foes, not His friends, controlled both incidents. Roman soldiers crucified Him with criminals. Pilate, the Roman governor, released His body to a rich man. The fulfillments of the prophecies were precise. He was buried according to the Scriptures.

John mentions four proofs that Jesus Christ actually died. The first indicator was John's eyewitness testimony. John said, "So when Jesus had received the sour wine, He said, 'It is finished!'[87] And bowing His head, He gave up His spirit."[88] John heard it and saw it. Jesus was dead.

The second evidence was the Roman soldier's affirmation of Jesus's surprisingly quick death. Crucifixion was a slow and painful death. The victims did not die of blood loss but of gradual agonizing suffocation.

The longer one hung on a cross the more difficult it was to breathe. The sufferer pushed up with his legs to expand his chest cavity, esophagus, and windpipe enough to take a breath. John recorded that the soldiers intended to speed up the three men's deaths. The Jews asked Pilate to break their legs so they could no longer lift their bodies to breathe. They did not want them hanging on the cross on the Passover preparation day. The soldiers broke the two thieves' legs but saw that Jesus was already dead. In fact, they fulfilled a prophecy when they did not break His legs.[89]

The mixture of blood and water that flowed out when a Roman soldier pierced His side is the third certain indicator of Jesus's death. "But one of the soldiers pierced his side with a spear, and immediately blood and water came out."[90]

Retired cardiothoracic surgeon, Dr. Antony de Bono, noted that due to the savage scourging, blood collected in Jesus's chest cavity before He died. After His death, Jesus's body hung on the cross for some time. As is normal, following death, accumulated blood separates. The heavier red cells sink to the bottom leaving a much lighter, straw colored plasma above. When the soldier's spear pierced His side, the red cells, which John describes as blood, gushes out first, followed by the plasma, which John described as water.[91]

The blood and water indicated that Jesus had already died when the spear pierced His side.

Finally, His burial was the fourth proof that Jesus was truly dead. The experienced Roman centurion and soldiers allowed His friends to take Him down from the cross because they knew He was dead. Those who took Him down knew He was dead as well. That's why they buried Him.

CHRIST ROSE FROM THE DEAD

Finally, "He rose again the third day according to the Scriptures."[92] Jesus defeated sin, death, and the grave. Without the resurrection, there is no Gospel.

After stating the three-fold content of the Gospel in 1 Corinthians 15:1-4, Paul invested the remainder of the chapter, the next fifty-four verses, demonstrating that Jesus Christ literally, physically, rose from the dead. Clearly the resurrection is essential to the Gospel.

Even in Paul's day, some denied the possibility of a resurrection. Paul declared, defended, and demonstrated Jesus's actual, physical, bodily resurrection.[93] It cannot be explained away as a hallucination induced by His followers' wishful thinking. Neither can Jesus's resurrection be spiritualized as in, "After His death and burial, Jesus lived on in the minds and hearts of the believers." These false explanations are pious denials of the resurrection. Both make the resurrection something that happened to His followers, rather than what happened to Jesus's physical body.

Seeing is Believing

Paul first noted multiple trustworthy and verifiable witnesses. They saw and interacted with Jesus. More than 514 members of the first century church saw Jesus alive and well after His resurrection.[94]

Not a Hopeless Hoax

Next, Paul declared the foolishness of faith in an un-resurrected Christ. Unless Jesus actually rose from the dead, Christianity is not a positive social influence or a commendable lifestyle option. If there is no resurrection, Christianity is a meaningless hoax. It promotes a hopeless faith and a miserable lifestyle. If Jesus Christ's resurrection was not real and actual, Christian preachers are liars and their converts are deceived.[95]

Paul affirmed, however, that the resurrection was real. Jesus rose because He truly died. He was not merely unconscious on the cross. He was not buried alive to later revive in the cool of the tomb. Jesus's death and resurrection were real. He was resurrected not resuscitated. This reality gives genuine hope.

Because Jesus defeated death and the grave, one day all believers will be raised and given glorified, resurrected bodies. Every believer will conquer the sting of death and celebrate the victory of eternal life in Jesus Christ. This victory inspires and motivates our faithfulness today. How? Our work for Him is not meaningless. Those who now trust Christ when we share the Gospel will live eternally; they too will be resurrected.[96]

CONCLUSION

Paul declared the Gospel. He emphasized that the Messiah's death, burial, and resurrection were not new innovations. They did not originate in Paul's creative mind. Rather, they were "according to the Scriptures." The New Testament Gospel is consistent with the Old Testament prophecies.

At this writing, the US academic community is placing renewed emphasis on mathematics. Many are concerned that the math skill of US graduates are lagging far behind the skills of graduates in other parts of the world. Elementary and secondary schools emphasize STEM education (Science, Technology, Engineering, and Math). Certainly it is important to enhance our students' math skills. Just don't do math with the Gospel!

The Gospel is a three-fold message. Christ died for our sins. Christ was buried. Christ rose from the dead. No element can be deleted without nullifying the true Gospel. Nothing can be added without diluting the true Gospel. Therefore, be faithful to the Bible's definition of the Gospel.

The **GOSPEL IS CRUCIAL**. Don't trivialize it. The **GOSPEL IS CLEAR**. Don't cloud it.

3

The Gospel Is

C E R T A I N

Through the years, I have been called for jury duty several times. I'm like most people. Seeing the 'Jury Summons' in the mail is not a welcome sight.

Jury duty is a major schedule disruption, but in the United States it's a part of citizenship. In that light, it is a privilege to serve, even if it doesn't feel like it while one is driving to the courthouse.

Serving on a jury can be a valuable learning experience. Here are a few useful nuggets I've picked up along the way.

A jury receives instructions about the laws related to the case before them. They also receive instructions about the rules of evidence. Various types of evidence carry more or less weight. For example, *circumstantial evidence* has the least weight. It can support a claim, but without additional evidence, it is insufficient to convict an accused. *Physical evidence*, particularly DNA evidence, carries great weight. An *expert witness* also carries great weight. *Eyewitness testimony* is one of the weightiest types of evidence.

The Apostle Paul understood evidence. As though he were a defense attorney, he presented his case for the certainty of the Gospel message and for the resurrection in particular. He began with the strongest kind of evidence. He presented more than 514 eyewitness testimonies.[97] Among these were three specific types of eyewitnesses. All had seen and interacted with Jesus after His resurrection.

First, Paul mentioned the Apostles. Second, he noted a large group. Third, he mentioned two transformed skeptics who refused to believe Jesus was the Christ until they saw Him alive. Consider these eyewitnesses.

THE TESTIMONY OF THE APOSTLES

First, Paul presented the testimonies of the Apostle Peter and "the twelve."[98] "The twelve" refers to the twelve Apostles, most likely including Mathias. The church chose him to replace Judas.[99] The eyewitness testimony of the Apostles is significant. A prior relationship with Jesus did not prejudice or discredit their testimonies. It strengthened their testimonies. It made them the most convincing eyewitnesses. Consider the facts.

The Apostles spent three years with Jesus Christ. They traveled with Him. They heard His sermons and saw His miracles. They knew Him up close and personal. Even so, His teaching often confounded them. They misunderstood and misinterpreted things He said and did.[100] Only after the resurrection did the things they had seen and heard suddenly click into place like the pieces of a puzzle.

When the soldiers arrested Jesus, most of the Apostles fled. Peter hung out in the background during a portion of Jesus's trial. Yet, when confronted, three times he denied that he knew Jesus.

John was the only disciple to stand by the cross. After Jesus's death, all of the Apostles, including John, hid out in an upper room.[101] The Apostles were not plotting a way to steal Jesus's body. They were not planning a vast conspiracy to convince gullible, superstitious people that Jesus was alive when they knew He was dead. They did not concoct the biggest hoax in history. Nothing could be further from the truth. The Apostles were discouraged, distressed, depressed, and afraid for their own lives.

When Jesus died on the cross, they did not expect Him to rise. They knew He was dead. They knew where He was buried. When they first heard that some women had seen Him alive, they didn't believe it.[102] They thought it was too good to be true. However, when they saw Him, talked to Him, touched Him, and ate with Him, they were convinced.[103] They knew it was their Lord Jesus. These men were certain about the resurrection, for they saw Him and talked with Him multiple times over a period of 40 days. They even saw Him ascend into the clouds. Jesus Christ personally chose the Apostles for a specific mission: they were witnesses "of His resurrection."[104]

After Jesus Christ rose from the dead and ascended to heaven, He fulfilled His promise to send the Holy Spirit.[105] Only then did the Apostles become bold witnesses. Nor was their boldness temporary.

Peter is an example. After he was Spirit filled on the day of Pentecost, he was fearless. He declared to a throng of Jewish listeners, "Therefore let all the house of Israel know assuredly that God has made this Jesus, whom you crucified, both Lord and Christ."[106]

Peter and John went to the temple. A man who had been lame since birth sat at the temple gate every day, begging. Peter and John had no money to give but they healed him in the name of Jesus. He went into the temple "walking, leaping, and praising God."[107]

A crowd quickly gathered. It included people who, just a few weeks earlier, demanded Jesus's crucifixion. This time Peter and John did not fear opposition. They did not run away or hide; they saw an opportunity. Peter said, "We didn't do this by our power. We did it in the name and by the power of Jesus Christ. God sent Him. You rejected Him and betrayed Him to Pilate.[108] 'But you denied the Holy One and the Just, ... and killed the Prince of life, whom God raised from the dead, of which we are witnesses.'"[109] Did you notice? At that strategic moment they proclaimed the Gospel—the death and resurrection of Jesus Christ.

Peter and John were arrested and threatened. The

Jewish Council ordered them "not to speak at all nor teach in the name of Jesus."[110] And how did these former self-protecting cowards respond? They said, "We cannot but speak the things which we have seen and heard."[111]

The Holy Spirit transformed the Apostles from fearful men, hiding from the Jewish leaders, into bold preachers. With wisdom and power they proclaimed the death, burial, and resurrection of Jesus Christ. As a result, the Apostles and many of the early believers faced arrest, imprisonment, beatings, torture, and death. History records that all the Apostles, with the possible exception of John, died a martyr's death. No wonder Paul began with the powerful eyewitness testimony of the Apostles.

THE TESTIMONY OF 500+

We also know that the resurrection is true and the Gospel is certain because of the testimony of more than 500 believers. Paul stated two significant realities about this large group of witnesses.

First, "He was seen by over five hundred brethren at once."[112] One day, during the 40 days between Jesus's resurrection and ascension, more than 500 believers gathered. We don't know where or why the group was gathered. Was it in a large house or by a river? Was it in Jerusalem, Bethany, or somewhere in Galilee? Were they there for a worship service? Had they gathered to discuss the latest news about Jesus's resurrection? We don't know any details about the event. We only know they were gathered, they were all believers, and someone counted them. Suddenly, Jesus was there with them. Whether He appeared out of thin air or walked into the midst of the group, they all saw Him. All knew it was Jesus. They knew He was not a ghost or spirit. He was there in the flesh. Alive.

A hallucination cannot explain this. One might have a hallucination. Two might have a similar hallucination. But more than 500 cannot have the same hallucination at the same time. Impossible.

Second, Paul noted that the "greater part remain to the present, but some have fallen asleep."[113] In other words, at the time Paul wrote 1 Corinthians, most of the people present at the event were still alive. Paul invited the readers to interview the eyewitnesses. There is no record of even one of the "over five hundred" believers recanting his or her testimony. All affirmed that the resurrection is true and the Gospel is certain.

THE TESTIMONY OF SKEPTICS

Finally, Paul gave the eyewitness testimonies of two transformed men. Before the resurrection, they were skeptics. After the resurrection, the Lord Jesus appeared to them and talked to them. Both men became faithful Gospel witnesses.

James

Paul called James to the witness stand. After the large crowd saw Jesus, Paul noted, "He was seen by James."[114] James was a popular name in New Testament times. It is "a form of the great Old Testament name Jacob."[115] The New Testament mentions at least four men named James.

1. James the son of Zebedee, brother of John
2. James the son of Alphaeus, also known as James the Less
3. James the father of Judas
4. James the half-brother of Jesus, also known as James the Just

The first two were among the twelve Apostles.[116] The third is obscure, only mentioned in Luke's list of the twelve, as the father of Judas. Whether or not he was one of Jesus's followers, we do not know. "Judas the son of James" distinguishes the faithful Apostle Judas from "Judas Iscariot who also became a traitor."[117]

In Paul's list of eyewitnesses, he separated this "James" from the twelve. We are 99.998% certain he was James the half-brother of Jesus.

Why is James significant? James and his brothers[118] were skeptical of Jesus during his earthly ministry. They did not believe He was the Messiah. They could not and would not believe they had grown up in the same home with the Messiah promised by the Old Testament prophets. When they learned to pray a Jewish man's morning prayers, which included a request for God to send the Messiah, they could not believe they were praying for their older brother's coming. They wrestled with Jesus. They swam with Jesus. He passed the soup at mealtimes and He slept on the mat next to theirs. How could He possibly be the One who would deliver Israel, reign over Israel, "speak peace to the nations," and have dominion "from sea to sea, and from the River to the ends of the earth"?[119]

It appears that, during Jesus's ministry, He was an embarrassment to His brothers and to people from His hometown. They thought He was delusional and out of His mind.[120] His brothers certainly were not among His followers.[121] They did not stand with Him during His trial nor were they with Him at the cross.

Things changed for James when He saw Jesus after the resurrection. After being an eyewitness of Christ's resurrection, James not only became a faithful believer, he became a "bondservant of Jesus."[122] James moved from being an unbelieving skeptic, to a faithful slave of Jesus the Christ, to the author of the New Testament book of James. The evidence in Acts points to his being the pastor of the Jerusalem church. In the final years of his life, James the Just was well known for his purity and his prayer life. He spent so many hours praying in the temple that his nickname was "Old Camel-Knees." Obviously he enjoyed intimate fellowship with his resurrected and ascended half-brother, Lord, and Savior. He remained faithful in spite of persecution and was martyred in approximately A.D. 62.[123] James never doubted Jesus's resurrection. He knew that Jesus was alive.

Paul

Last but not least, Paul stepped away from the lawyer's lectern. He sat in the witness chair to add his own testimony to the record. "Then last of all," Paul said, "He was seen by me also, as one born out of due time."[124]

It is very likely that Paul was at Jesus's trial. He was a Pharisee of the Pharisees. He was brought up at the feet of Gamaliel. He had access to the Sanhedrin. At any rate, we know that Paul spent all his efforts and energy to persecute Jesus's early followers. He was more than an outspoken skeptic; he was an active persecutor—"breathing threats and murder against the disciples of the Lord."[125]

Paul was radically transformed from an angry skeptic into a servant of Christ. The persecutor became a preacher.

What caused the radical transformation? He met the living, resurrected Lord Jesus on the road to Damascus. Paul recognized and surrendered to Jesus's Lordship. Another skeptic became a bondservant of Jesus Christ.[126]

We too know the Gospel is certain. We believe the trustworthy testimony of God's Word. The valid and verifiable, true and trustworthy eyewitness testimonies of the twelve Apostles assure us. We trust the testimony of a group of more than 500 who saw the resurrected Lord Jesus at the same time. We also have the testimony of two first century skeptics who became unflinching followers of Christ.

CONTEMPORARY TRANSFORMATIONS

The Gospel of Jesus Christ remains powerful after nearly 2000 years. Wherever the Gospel is proclaimed, it still transforms the fearful and the faithless into faithful followers of Jesus Christ.

The Gospel is the need of nominal, cultural Christians. It answers honest agnostics. It is spiritual balm for bitter atheists. The true Gospel, honestly examined, will convict, convert, and transform the one who believes in the death, burial, and resurrection of the Biblical Lord Jesus Christ.

Lew Wallace

Lew Wallace was something of a Renaissance man. He was a lawyer, newspaper reporter, inventor, biographer, novelist, Union Army officer in the War Between the States, and more. He left the army in 1865. President Rutherford B. Hayes appointed him Governor of the New Mexico Territory (1878-81). President James Garfield appointed him to serve as the

U.S. Minister to the Ottoman Empire (1881-85). His true claim to fame, however, was being the author of, *Ben-Hur: A Tale of the Christ*. It became the best-selling book and the most influential Christian book of the 19th century.

Wallace grew up in Indiana. His home, schools, and Indiana communities respected the Christian tradition. He considered himself a Christian. Wallace was never an atheist, as is sometimes reported. However, when his nominal faith was challenged, he did not know how to respond. He was humiliated.[127] Carol Wallace, his great great granddaughter, told how it happened. She wrote:

> In 1876, Lew found himself in a train compartment with Robert Ingersoll, a superstar of the day—a sought-after speaker and America's foremost agnostic. Ingersoll enjoyed grilling new acquaintances about their faith.
>
> Lew had considered himself a Christian, but he didn't go to church, didn't pray regularly and barely knew the Bible. He was embarrassed by Ingersoll's questions.[128]

In his Autobiography, published posthumously in 1906, he noted the spiritual condition that his conversation with Ingersoll unveiled. He wrote, "At that time, speaking candidly, I was not in the least influenced by religious sentiment. I had no convictions about God or Christ. I neither believed nor disbelieved in them." He realized he was unacquainted with the faith he claimed. He knew nothing about basic Christian beliefs such as "God, heaven, life hereafter, Jesus Christ and His divinity."[129]

"He felt he should know more about his faith. And he decided that the best way to educate himself would be to write a novel set at the time of Christ, about a young man whose life is changed by Jesus."[130] Over the next three years, as he researched and wrote *Ben-Hur*, Lew Wallace came to personal faith in Jesus Christ. He later said that, "through the research and writing of *Ben-Hur*, by learning of the story of Christ, 'I found myself writing reverentially, and frequently with awe.' So although Wallace never intended *Ben-Hur* to be a debunking of Christianity, he still found himself transfixed, and transformed, by the life of Jesus Christ."[131]

"Lew Wallace spoke frequently about the conversation with Robert Green Ingersoll that led him to write *Ben-Hur*, and he maintained throughout his life that the experience of writing the novel led him gradually to accept the basic tenets of the Christian Gospel."[132] When one hears and understands the true Gospel, it has the power to convict, convert, and transform.

Josh McDowell

Josh McDowell is one of today's best-known Christian authors, speakers, and apologists. He has authored and co-authored 151 books. These have been translated into 128 languages. He has addressed 46,000,000 people, giving more than 27,200 talks in 139 countries. However, as a young man, McDowell:

> ... considered himself an agnostic. He truly believed that Christianity was worthless. However, when challenged to intellectually examine the claims of Christianity, Josh discovered compelling, overwhelming evidence for the reliability of the Christian faith. After trusting in Jesus Christ as Savior and Lord, Josh's life changed dramatically as he experienced the power of God's love.[133]

Lee Strobel

Lee Strobel was an atheist and an award-winning journalist for the *Chicago Tribune*. When his wife began to attend a local church and study the Bible with other ladies, he was disappointed. When she believed the Gospel and received Christ, he was angry. He determined to rescue her from her obviously naïve religious deception. He determined to do an extended journalistic investigation of the Christian faith. He was confident he could prove, once and for all, that Bible based Christianity is an intellectual house of cards. He would easily bring it tumbling down. To his great shock, however, his investigation proved the opposite.

Strobel realized his own atheistic faith was intellectually indefensible. It, not Biblical faith, was the house of cards; and it tumbled down around him. He discovered that the Bible is true, believable, and verifiable. He learned that Jesus Christ was indeed God in the flesh. He died on a cross, was buried, and rose from the dead. Like Lew Wallace and Josh McDowell before him, Strobel discovered the Biblical Gospel and surrendered his heart and life to Jesus Christ. He published his investigation and salvation testimony in the best selling book, *The Case for Christ*.[134] Since his conversion, Strobel's "life work has been to share the evidence that supports the truth and claims of Christianity and to equip believers to share their faith with the people they know and love." He has authored and co-authored more than twenty books that give a firm defense of Biblical faith.[135]

Each of these men honestly searched for truth. Each began from a different perspective. Each followed the evidence where it led. An atheist, like Strobel, believes there is no God to know. An agnostic, like McDowell, believes that if there is a God, he or she is unknowable. A nominal, cultural Christian, like Wallace, unaware of his own ignorance, imagines he already knows God. But no matter where each began, the Gospel was the ultimate answer for all three.

CONCLUSION

The **GOSPEL IS CRUCIAL**. It is the only message that can save from sin. It is the only message that brings sinners into a right relationship with God. No other message can give one the assurance of having a home in heaven.

The **GOSPEL IS CLEAR**. Its three-fold content exclusively includes:

- Christ died for our sins according to the Scriptures.
- Christ was buried.
- Christ rose again the third day according to the Scriptures.

When Jesus Christ died and rose, He defeated sin, the grave, and death.

The **GOSPEL IS CERTAIN**. We have the testimony of the twelve, the testimony of a group of over 500, and the testimony of skeptics.

Finally, for me, the Gospel's cruciality, clarity, and certainty are personal. When I was a young teen, my pastor and home church in Pueblo, Colorado, infused me with a passion to get the Gospel right and never alter its content. One particular event made a life-transforming impact on me.

My pastor invited a guest preacher to our church. I don't remember his name, but I have never forgotten a story he told. It challenges and motivates me to this very day. He said:

One night I had a dream. In my dream I looked into hell. I saw countless people suffering in the flames. Many cried out, "Why did I reject Jesus? Why didn't I listen to my family, my friends, and all those who told me how to be saved from this horrible place?"

A man walked through the flames searching one face after another. He stopped each person he came to and stared into his or her eyes. When he saw it wasn't the person he wanted to see, he moved on, groping through the flames and the darkness. When he stumbled upon people who had fallen, he grabbed them by the hair and lifted them up. He looked into their eyes, dropped them, and moved on."

"As he came near me," the preacher said, "I asked what he was doing. The man looked at me and said, 'I'm looking for the preacher who told me I would be OK. He told me I didn't need to worry about hell.'"

I was a young teenage preacher when I heard that story. That day, I was deeply convicted. I determined to never be "that" preacher. Those who will hear me preach and teach cannot afford for me to get the Gospel wrong. I cannot play math with the Gospel, adding to it or subtracting from it. I must proclaim the Gospel as defined in the Scriptures. No other Gospel will do.

Likewise, I am eternally grateful for those who shared the Biblical Gospel with me. I'm thankful they didn't play math with the Gospel. Neither did they dumb it down. I was very young, but it was critical for me to hear the true Gospel. That's really where this little book began.

4

The Gospel Is

SERIOUS

It is easy to identify first time fliers. When the flight attendant says, "Would you please take the flight information card from the back of the seat in front of you and follow along as I explain the safety features of our aircraft," the first time fliers are the ones who actually take out the card and listen to the briefing. The rest of us have heard it all before—word for word. Who cares about the emergency exits, flotation devices, and oxygen masks? Besides, is there anyone in America who doesn't know how to latch and release a seatbelt?

May I Have Your Attention Please

If, however, in mid-flight the pilot announced, "I regret to inform you that two of our engines have malfunctioned; a third is on fire. We must make an emergency ocean landing. Please take the flight information card from the back of the seat in front of you and follow along ... " I'm confident the interest level would rise.

You Have My Attention,
But I'm Not Pleased

That was certainly true for me when I was five years old. Don't misunderstand. I wasn't in a mid-flight mishap. It was worse than that and the distress lasted much longer. The two most miserable years of my life were between the ages of 5 and 7. Let me explain.

I grew up in a Christian home, the youngest of nine children. Every day my parents read the Bible and led each of us in prayer. They never sent us to church; they took us. Furthermore, they followed the 'three-to-thrive principle.' Our family was in church three times every week: Sunday morning, Sunday night, and Wednesday night. Whenever a Bible-believing church in our area held revival services, we were there as well. Before I learned to read, my parents and siblings taught me to memorize Scripture. But none of that—Bible reading, prayer, faithful church attendance, or Scripture memory—alleviated my misery. It just made it worse.

In a Sunday morning worship service as our pastor preached, God's Spirit convicted me of my sin. It was sudden and shocking. I realized that my family members were Christians, but I was not. I realized I was lost and headed for hell. The rest of my family was saved and headed for heaven. I would be separated from all of them—forever. I assure you, that wasn't a comfortable thought for a five year old.

For me, it was like a pilot announcing, "I regret to inform you ..." Certain disaster was approaching, but I knew there was hope. I knew there was a way for me to avoid the disaster. Jesus could and would change my destiny. I simply had to trust Him.

I understood that Jesus was God's eternal Son. He came to earth as a human. He was tempted but He never sinned. I realized that Jesus loves me so much that when He died on the cross He received the punishment I deserve. I understood that He was buried and that He rose from the dead. I realized that if I turned to Him asking Him to forgive me, if I trusted Jesus to be my Lord and Savior, I would be forgiven. I too would be a real Christian.

Notice something important. I, a five year old, believed the true-Gospel facts. Children can understand a clear presentation of the Biblical Gospel. The message can be clarified and simplified, but it doesn't have to be dumbed down for them. In fact, it must not be. Children can understand far more than "Jesus loves you and you should love Him too." If children believe a sentimental, bloodless, semi-Gospel, they believe a false Gospel. By the way, the same is true for teenagers and adults.

When the sermon ended, the conviction became even stronger. We stood to sing an invitation hymn. The pastor invited all who were willing to receive Jesus to come to the front of the Church and publicly profess their faith in Jesus.

The Negotiator

At that point I knew what to do. I knew I needed to trust Jesus Christ to save me. I knew I must receive Him, but for some reason I resisted Him. I told God, "I'll receive Jesus someday, but not now. I want to just be a kid, have fun, and do what I want with my life." I wanted the benefits of salvation:

· Heaven,
· No separation from my family.

But I wanted the benefits on my own terms.

Can you imagine such arrogance? Why would a five year old in Colorado think he had the right to open negotiations for his soul with the eternal, almighty God in heaven?

The invitation continued.

I looked up and saw Eddie coming down the aisle. He walked past our pew on his way to talk to the pastor. I knew Eddie well. He was a friend of my older brothers. Eddie was 12 years old. At that moment I was inspired, but not in the right way. I didn't follow his example; I used him as a negotiating tool. "God," I promised, "I'll trust Jesus when I'm 12 like Eddie." The service ended and I couldn't wait to get out of there!

Thus began the two most miserable years of my life. I began two years of:

- Running from God.
- Resisting the Holy Spirit's conviction.
- Regularly trying to negotiate a truce with God ("If you'll stop making me feel guilty, I'll get saved soon, or maybe when I'm 12.")

Sound familiar? Did you have a similar experience? Are you enduring a similar misery right now?

Jesus's Answer for Negotiators

Jesus has an answer for arrogant five-year-old negotiators. In fact, it is His answer for spiritual negotiators of any age. He said, "Most assuredly, I say to you, he who hears My word and believes in Him who sent Me has everlasting life, and shall not come into judgment, but has passed from death into life."[136] This is good news; it is Gospel news. Everlasting life is available to anyone who will accept it on Jesus's terms. No debate. No negotiations.

Salvation is a gift of grace, not a negotiation. The Gospel is not a cafeteria line where you select the content items you want and leave the rest. Nor is the Gospel a file folder from which you remove the items you don't want and add items you do want. We cannot compromise the true Gospel of salvation through Jesus Christ without changing its content and its consequent results. The Biblical Gospel—nothing more, nothing less—is serious.

TRUTH YOU CAN TRUST

Jesus began, "Most assuredly," literally, *amen*, *amen* or truly, truly. Both the Greek and English words are transliterations of the Hebrew word. Sometimes it is translated "truth" as in the God of *amen*, "the God of truth." We use it at the end of our prayers, "meaning truly, surely, certainly.[137]... In the entire New Testament, only the Lord Jesus uses *amen* at the beginning of a sentence.... Throughout the Gospel of John, the Lord uses the word *amen*, doubled."[138] You can believe whatever Jesus says without a doubt.

One morning a friend received an email he thought was from me. The email asked him to do a personal favor. The summary of multiple email exchanges was, "I'm in a meeting so I can't call you. I want to honor three faculty members with a surprise gift. Can you go to a store and buy three $100 Amazon gift cards? Scratch off the code numbers on the back. Take a picture of the three cards and email it to me." Because we know one another well, my friend did not think this was something I would ask him to do.

He answered, "I can do that, but I'll have to speak to you first. Call me."

He then sent a text to me. He asked if I had made the request. "No," I said. "I have an imposter." Verifying the source saved my friend from sending $300 to a liar and a thief.

In our day when many no longer value truth, it is refreshing to hear that some things are truly, most assuredly, true. In John's Gospel Jesus declared no less than 24 times, "Amen, amen, I say to you." When multiple frauds and liars prey on the trusting and unsuspecting, it is wonderful to know that our God does not lie. We can trust Him because He is "the God of truth"[139] and, therefore, the "God who cannot lie."[140]

HEAR GOD'S WORD

Our Lord Jesus's non-negotiable answer for spiritual negotiators is, "Most assuredly, I say to you, he who hears My word ... has everlasting life." The person who receives everlasting life must first "hear" God's Word. You realize, of course, that hearing God's Word doesn't simply refer to hearing the Bible read aloud.

When you ask your children, "Did you hear me?" you aren't questioning the functioning of their ears. You want to know if they were paying attention and intend to obey your instructions. Likewise, when Jesus says, "Hear My word," He insists that we pay attention, that we believe and obey His Word.

It isn't necessary to have extensive Bible knowledge before you can receive everlasting life. There are, however, basic truths you must know and believe.

Your Sin

First, you must believe what the Bible says about your sin. "For all have sinned and fall short of the glory of God."[141] *You are a sinner.*

"Sin" is "missing the mark."[142] Picture an arrow missing a target. The target is perfect obedience to God's law. Jesus said, "Therefore you shall be perfect, just as your Father in heaven is perfect."[143] No one but the Lord Jesus has ever hit that target.

The arrows are our thoughts, words, and deeds. When we shoot at the target our arrows hit the ground instead of the target. We sin. Our thoughts, words, and deeds "fall short of the glory of God." This is why we need the Biblical Gospel. "Christ died," not simply as an example of self-sacrificial service or as a martyr for a cause, but "for our sins."[144]

We all need Christ's sacrifice because everyone is a sinner, including you and me. "There is none righteous, no, not one."[145] Realizing that, some ask, "So what? Everyone is in the same boat. What difference does it make?" I don't know about you but I don't find any comfort in the fact that we are all in a sinking boat.

The Bible also says we are *separated from God.* "The wages of sin is death."[146] Our sin earns eternal separation from God. Unless something drastic happens, every sinner will be separated from God forever in hell.[147]

A sinner, separated from God, is *unable to earn sal-*

vation. Frankly, most people don't believe that. Most live with the confidence that someday, somehow they will earn their salvation. Heaven will be their eternal home because they deserve it.

In contrast, God said that no amount of good works, church attendance, baptism, or Bible reading will take a sinner to heaven. "Therefore by the deeds of the law no flesh will be justified in His sight."[148] Without this reality, the Gospel is not serious. If you are not a sinner, you do not need a Savior.

But here is the fact. We are sinners. It's in the first essential tenet of the Gospel: "Christ died for our sins."

Do you believe what God said about your sin? If so, you are beginning to hear the Word of God. He said you are a sinner, separated from Him, and unable to save yourself.

Your Savior

Second, you must hear God's Word about your Savior, Jesus Christ. He was *God in the flesh*. The Bible says, "In the beginning was the Word, and the Word was with God, and the Word was God.... And the Word became flesh and dwelt among us, and we beheld His glory, the glory as of the only begotten of the Father."[149] The most famous verse in the Bible confirms the identity of "the only begotten" who "became flesh." "For God so loved the world that He gave His only begotten Son."[150] Jesus Christ was the eternal sinless God in a human body.

When Jesus died on the cross, He was *punished for our sins.* The sinless One suffered for all the sinful ones. Peter described Jesus as the One "'who committed no sin, nor was deceit found in His mouth' ... who Himself bore our sins in His own body on the tree."[151]

Again, it's in the first essential tenet of the Gospel: It was "Christ," the Messiah, who "died for our sins." Because His sacrifice provides the gift of everlasting life for all who receive Him, the Gospel is serious. I understood this when I was 5, 6, and 7. How? I had heard the Biblical Gospel over and over.

Your Salvation

To have everlasting life you must hear God's Word about your sin, your Savior, and third, your salvation. The Bible says sinners are saved *by grace.* "For by grace you have been saved through faith, and that not of yourselves; *it is* the gift of God, not of works, lest anyone should boast."[152]

Grace is God's favor that you did not earn and do not deserve. Someone described it with an acrostic: God's Riches At Christ's Expense.

God's riches: forgiveness, heaven, eternal life, peace, joy, and a sense of the love of God—at Christ's expense. The expense of the scourge, Gethsemane, the mocking, the plucking of his beard, the crown of thorns, the nailing of his hands, the piercing on his side, the wrath of God, and hell itself. "Jesus paid it all. All to Him I owe." He offers us eternal life as a gift by grace.[153]

The Bible teaches that sinners are saved by grace *through faith.* "For by grace you have been saved through faith ... not of works."[154] Faith trusts God for everlasting life rather than trusting in self and good works.

Sinners are saved by grace through faith, and it is *a gift of God.* We can never earn salvation but we can receive the gift of salvation. Someone said, "Faith is the hand of a beggar receiving the gift of a king."[155]

I understood these simple facts during my two miserable years, but I refused to reach out. I refused to receive the gift of everlasting life. I was determined to be in control and do what I wanted when I wanted.

God was gracious and persistent. Every church service, even though I dug in my heels, the Holy Spirit's conviction continued. I began to dread going to church. I wanted God to stop bothering me because I was years away from 12.

Jesus said, "To have everlasting life, you must hear My Word." You can accept what God says about your sin, your Savior, and your salvation. This is the good news of the Gospel.

Your Two Parents

Just as we have two parents when we are born, we also have two parents when we are born again: the Spirit of God[156] and the Word of God.[157] The Spirit of God uses the Word of God to lead us to faith in the Son of God and He gives us the life of God—we are born from above.[158]

The Holy Spirit works when and where the Word is faithfully proclaimed. Jesus said that the Holy Spirit would "convict the world of sin, and of righteousness, and of judgment."[159] Not believing in Jesus is the chief sin for which the Holy Spirit convicts.[160] The Spirit and the Word work together to convict and convert sinners. I didn't understand the theology when I was 5, but I sure did experience the reality.

Over time our church experienced difficulties. People began leaving. The pastor was at odds with a significant number of people. I didn't understand it as a kid, but I knew the miserable conviction stopped. It made me comfortable; I really didn't mind going to church then.

Soon my parents also began looking for a new church. We would visit a church for a few Sundays and then return to our old church. I noticed something. When we went to our old church there was no conviction. I could sit through the Sunday School lesson and the sermon without a problem. When we went to other churches the conviction returned. I hated to visit other churches.

My seat in the family station wagon was in the very back. When we loaded into the car to go to church, Dad didn't tell us our destination. He just drove.

I knew that when we came to a certain intersection, if we turned right we were going to our old church. If we turned left, we were going to visit a new church. Right meant comfort. Left meant conviction.

As we approached that intersection each Sunday, I was in the back watching and praying. For me it became "Intercession Intersection." It was fervent intercession but it was fruitless. "Lord," I pleaded, "please let us go to our old church today!" I smiled when we turned right. I was sad when we turned left.

BELIEVE IN JESUS CHRIST

To have everlasting life, faith in Jesus Christ must follow hearing the Word. Jesus said, "Most assuredly, I say to you, he who hears My word and believes in Him who sent Me."

The Word is Necessary

Hearing the Word is necessary because "faith comes by hearing and hearing by the word of God."[161] Faith, the ability to trust and believe, is a part of the image of God in every person.[162] A child can believe as well as a teenager or an adult. After all, a child's trust is the example for adults, not the other way around. "Then

Jesus called a little child to Him, set him in the midst of them, and said, 'Assuredly, I say to you, unless you are converted and become as little children, you will by no means enter the kingdom of heaven.'"[163]

The Word and the Spirit awaken God-implanted faith in your heart and focuses it on Jesus Christ alone. Whether your faith is dead or alive, non-saving or saving depends on the object of your faith. If your faith is in yourself, a church, good works, a fine family, rule keeping, baptism, or religious rituals, it is dead faith. It will not save. If, however, your faith is focused on Jesus Christ alone for your salvation, your faith is alive; it is saving faith. Living faith is in a living Lord. To state the obvious, this is in the third Gospel tenet. Jesus Christ is alive because He who died for our sins and was buried "rose again the third day."[164]

After hearing the Word, if one "believes in Him who sent Me," he or she will be saved. Who sent Jesus? "The Father ... sent Him."[165] Does that contradict, "Believe on the Lord Jesus Christ, and you will be saved"[166]? No, not at all. If anyone truly believes in the Father, he or she also believes in the Son. Jesus said, "I and My Father are one."[167]

It is impossible to receive the Father and reject the Son. "Whoever denies the Son does not have the Father either; he who acknowledges the Son has the Father also."[168]

THE RESULTS OF HEARING
AND BELIEVING

Next, Jesus stated the results of hearing and believing. "Most assuredly, I say to you, he who hears My word and believes in Him who sent Me has everlasting life, and shall not come into judgment, but has passed from death into life."

Everlasting Life

The first promised result: the one who "hears ... and believes ... has everlasting life." One has spiritual life that never ends. Notice that it is a present tense promise, not future. Everlasting life is a present possession with a guarantee that does not expire. You now have and you will continue to have everlasting life.

Someone may ask, "Are you suggesting that saved people can never lose their salvation?"

"Not only am I suggesting it, I'm stating it."

"But what if a believer commits a really bad sin, then dies before he can confess it? Would he still go to heaven?"

"Yes. Good morals do not save us nor do they maintain our salvation. Jesus Christ saves us and keeps us saved. Whether one is entering or continuing the Christian life, 'the blood of Jesus Christ His Son cleanses us from all sin'[169] Jesus guaranteed, 'All that the Father gives Me will come to Me, and the one who comes to Me I will by no means cast out.'"[170]

Sinners enter God's family when we hear God's Word, and believe upon and receive God's Son. "But as many as received Him, to them He gave the right to become children of God, to those who believe in His name."[171]

No Condemnation

The good news continues. The one who hears and believes "shall not come into judgment." The Apostle Paul celebrated the same good news. He said, "There is therefore now no condemnation[172] to those who are in Christ Jesus."[173]

Satan condemns those Jesus cleanses.[174] But we do not fear Satan's condemnation. The Judge of all the earth is on our side. "For the Father judges no one, but has committed all judgment to the Son."[175] Therefore Paul asked, "Who shall bring a charge against God's elect? *It is* God who justifies. Who *is* he who condemns? *It is* Christ who died, and furthermore is also risen, who is even at the right hand of God, who also makes intercession for us."[176] If that gives you confidence, I'm glad. It should.

Death into Life

Finally, the one who hears and believes "has passed from death into life." Spiritual death is our natural

condition. The un-forgiven sinner is dead in tres-
passes and sins and therefore unable to redeem himself.[177] Jesus, however, does for us what we cannot do
for ourselves. He promises, "Most assuredly, I say to
you, the hour is coming, and now is, when the dead
will hear the voice of the Son of God; and those who
hear will live."[178]

When one hears the Word and receives Jesus by
faith, God gives eternal life instantly. He rescues us
from the kingdom of death and darkness and trans-
fers us into His kingdom of life, light, and love. As
Paul stated, "He has delivered us from the power of
darkness and conveyed *us* into the kingdom of the
Son of His love, in whom we have redemption through
His blood, the forgiveness of sins."[179]

All of this seems too grand and amazing to happen
to a passively rebellious seven-year-old boy in Pueblo,
Colorado. But I can assure you it happened to me.

My parents found a new church home for our family. If they had asked for my vote, they would not
have joined First Southern Baptist Church in Pueblo,
Colorado. I didn't like it at all. It had three major
faults. The church was unified, the pastor preached
the Word, and the Holy Spirit was working.

My conviction and misery returned and intensi-
fied. I hated going to our new church, but my parents
took me anyway. Now, 45 years later, I sure am glad.

One day in May of 1975 my two years of running
and resisting, negotiating and procrastinating finally
ended. I was sitting all alone in the living room of our

house. I assure you, with 12 people living in our small house, it was rare. I don't really know how or why I was alone, but I was. Christian music was playing in the background and the Holy Spirit began convicting my heart. I thought, "This is serious. I'm under conviction and I'm not even at church."

Finally my resistance weakened and collapsed. I was 7 years old and I surrendered. I turned to the Lord Jesus in prayer. Right there, all alone in the living room, I trusted Jesus to be my Lord and Savior. Instantly the misery broke. A joy and peace I had never known flooded over me. And the truth is, it didn't wear off. Even as I tell you about it today I feel that same joy and peace.

The following Sunday, May 18, 1975, the Spirit of God prompted me to respond to our pastor's invitation. That day I made a public profession of faith. A few Sundays later I followed the Lord in believer's baptism.

Someone may ask, "Mark, why did you wait so long? Why did you resist?"

Looking Back

In retrospect, I'm grateful for God's grace. He was patient and persistent with a young rebel. I'm also impressed by the accurate and applicable insight in God's Word. As if reading my heart from across the years and miles, the prophet Jeremiah diagnosed my resistance. He said, "The heart *is* deceitful above all *things,* and desperately wicked; who can know it?"[180]

Even though my heart was sinful, God was merciful. He continued to convict me of the sin of not receiving Jesus.[181] The day I surrendered my will, the Spirit of God took the Word of God and led me to the Son of God. When I trusted Him, I received everlasting life instead of judgment. I passed from death into life.

Looking Forward

If that has never happened to you, it can. You don't need to run and resist for two years. You can trust Jesus Christ right now.

Do you feel the need to have your sins cleansed? Do you believe Jesus Christ was punished for your sins when He died on the cross? Do you believe that three days after He was buried He actually rose from the dead? Do you believe He conquered sin, death, and the grave? Then you believe the true Gospel facts. You need to do only one more thing.

"For '*whoever calls* on the name of the Lord shall be saved.'"[182] Will you call on Him right now? Reach out to Him in faith. Believe on Him. Receive Him now. Here is a sample prayer. If it expresses your heart's desire, pray it to God.

"Heavenly Father, I know I am a sinner. I know I cannot save myself. I know I deserve to be eternally separated from You."

"I believe you love me and sent Jesus Christ to be

punished for my sins. I believe He died on the cross in my place, was buried, and rose from the dead three days later. You promised that if I would receive Him, You would take away my sins and give me everlasting life. You said, 'Call,' so I am calling. Lord Jesus I come to You through faith. Please forgive all my sins and be my Lord and Savior. I trust You now."

"Thank You Father for hearing my prayer and saving me now. Help me to live for you. In Jesus's name, Amen."

Did you just now pray that or a similar prayer? Did you believe on and receive Jesus Christ? If so, He saved you and gave you eternal life. Let me be the first to say, "Welcome to the family of God!"

And so we end where we began—with the Gospel. I hope it is crystal clear why words and their definitions matter. I trust you see why I am convinced: **THE GOSPEL IS CRUCIAL**, **THE GOSPEL IS CLEAR**, **THE GOSPEL IS CERTAIN**, and **THE GOSPEL IS SERIOUS**.

If you received Jesus after reading this book, I would be honored if you would tell me. If you have further questions or need help finding a Bible-believing and teaching church near you, please contact me, Mark Ballard, at m.ballard@nebcvt.org. I, or one of my staff members, will contact you promptly. We will be happy to help. In the meantime, share the Gospel with someone else.

NOTES

1. Mark 1:14-15; See also Acts 15:7; Romans 1:16

2. Spirios Zodhiates, *The Complete Word Study Dictionary: New Testament*, electronic ed. (Chattanooga, TN: AMG Publishers, 2000), s.v., "εὐαγγέλιον, *euaggélion*."

3. Ibid.

4. 1 Corinthians 15:1, 3-4

5. R. Scott Clark, "Why Complementarianism Can't Be a 'Gospel' Issue"; accessed 14 June 2020, https://heidelblog.net/2012/09/why-complementarianism-cant-be-a-Gospel-issue/.

6. Ibid.

7. James 1:27

8. Matthew 22:37-39

9. Phil Johnson, "A Gospel Issue?" accessed 11 June 2020, https://statementonsocialjustice.com/articles/Gospel-issue/.

10. Ibid.

11. Ibid.

12. For whoever shall keep the whole law, and yet stumble in one *point,* he is guilty of all (James 2:10).

13. Therefore the law was our tutor *to bring us* to Christ, that we might be justified by faith (Gal 3:24).

14. Therefore by the deeds of the law no flesh will be justified in His sight, for by the law *is* the knowledge of sin (Rom 3:20). Knowing that a man is not justified by the works of the law but by faith in Jesus Christ, even we have believed in Christ Jesus, that we might be justified by faith in Christ and not by the works of the law; for by the works of the law no flesh shall be justified (Galatians 2:16).

15. Matthew 22:37

16. Matthew 22:39

17. A false teaching that denies a number of traditional Christian doctrines, including the Trinity and Christ's deity, and affirms that salvation is given to those who adopt Christ's values. See *Dictionary.com*, s.v., "Socinian", accessed 7 July 2020; also, Everett F. Harrison, Geoffrey W. Bromiley, and Carl F. H. Henry, eds., *Baker's Dictionary of Theology* (Grand Rapids: Baker Book House, 1960), s.v., "Socinianism." It teaches the Example Theory of the Atonement, denying "that God's justice re-

quires payment for sin; it says that Christ's death simply provides us with an example of how we should trust and obey God perfectly, even if that trust and obedience leads to a horrible death." Wayne Grudem, *Systematic Theology: An Introduction to Biblical Doctrine* (Grand Rapids: Zondervan, 1994), 582.

18. "A belief system based on the principle that people's spiritual and emotional needs can be satisfied without following a god or religion." *Cambridge Dictionary*, s.v., "Humanism" in https://dictionary.cambridge.org/dictionary/english/humanism, accessed 7 July 2020.

19. Phil Johnson, "A Gospel Issue?"

20. Ibid.

21. See Acts 15:1-5; Galatians 2:11-14; 5:1-6

22. Zodhiates, *Word Study Dictionary*, s.v., "ἕτερος, *héteros*."

23. Ibid., s.v., "ἄλλος, *állos*."

24. Galatians 1:6-9

25. Galatians 5:9

26. 1 Corinthians 15:1-2

27. Acts 1:8

28. Hebrews 10:23-25

29. 1 Corinthians 15:1

30. 1 Corinthians 15:2

31. Zodhiates, *Word Study Dictionary*, "κατέχω, *katéchō*."

32. 1 Corinthians 15:3

33. Warren W Wiersbe, *The Bible Exposition Commentary*: NT, vol. 1 (Wheaton, IL: Victor Books, 1996), 617.
34. Acts 16:30-32
35. Acts 17:18
36. Acts 23:6
37. "To take to oneself, seize or take into one's possession." Zodhiates, *Word Study Dictionary*, s.v., "παραλαμβάνω, *paralambánō.*"
38. Romans 3:23
39. Matthew 5:48
40. Romans 6:23; Exodus 34:12
41. Psalm 51:10, 14
42. "*Catamites*, those submitting to homosexuals"—NKJV marginal note
43. "Male homosexuals"—NKJV marginal note
44. 1 Corinthians 6:9-10—Paul's list of sins describes every present day major city in the world. Corinth's sins are no longer notorious; they are the norm.
45. 1 Corinthians 6:10
46. 1 Corinthians 6:11
47. 1 Corinthians 15:1-2
48. Pure and undefiled religion before God and the Father is this: to visit orphans and widows in their trouble, *and* to keep oneself unspotted from the world (James 1:27).
49. Acts 18:2
50. Romans 1:15-16

51. Acts 15
52. Ephesians 3:6
53. Ephesians 2:11–13
54. Philemon 16
55. 1 Corinthians 2:1-5
56. Romans 6:23
57. 1 Corinthians 15:3-4
58. Isaiah 7:14; 9:6; Micah 5:2
59. Isaiah 53:9-10; 1 Corinthians 15:3-4
60. Isaiah 53:10
61. Jesus was crucified between two criminals (Luke 23:23). He was buried in a rich man's tomb (Luke 23:50-55; Isaiah 53:9).
62. The Messiah's death will be vicarious and sacrificial.
63. He who died will see His seed and prolong His days because He will rise from the dead (Isaiah 53:10).
64. Genesis 3:1-19
65. Luke 23:33
66. Genesis 3:15
67. Luke 1:34-37; The three alliterated points on this page are inspired by a sermon preached by Adrian Rogers during his early years at Bellevue Baptist Church. I originally heard the sermon on an audio cassette tape in 1977 or 78.
68. M. G. Easton, *Easton's Bible Dictionary* (New York: Harper & Brothers, 1893), s.v. "Enmity."

69. John 12:31-33; 1 Corinthians 2:6-8; Colossians 2:14-15
70. Revelation 21:10
71. Ezekiel 18:4, 20
72. Romans 6:23
73. Genesis 3:15; Matthew 1:21
74. John 3:16; Matthew 5:48
75. 1 Timothy 2:5; 1 John 5:20
76. John 1:14
77. Hebrews 4:15
78. Romans 6:23
79. Genesis 2:15-17
80. "So when the woman saw that the tree *was* good for food, that it *was* pleasant to the eyes, and a tree desirable to make *one* wise, she took of its fruit and ate. She also gave to her husband with her, and he ate" (Genesis 3:6).
81. Genesis 5:5
82. Romans 5:12
83. Romans 1:18
84. 1 John 4:14
85. Isaiah 53:9
86. Matthew 27:38, 57-61
87. It is finished is one word in Greek—*tetelestai*—paid in full. Jesus did not say, "I am finished" but "sins debt is paid in full.
88. John 19:30
89. Psalm 34:20; John 19:31-33, 36
90. John 19:34

91. Kathleen N. Hattrup, "A doctor on why "blood and water" gushed from Jesus' heart", accessed 11 July 2020; https://aleteia.org/2019/06/22/a-doctor-on-why-blood-and-water-gushed-from-jesus-heart/.

92. 1 Corinthians 15:4

93. 1 Corinthians 15:5-58

94. 1 Corinthians 15:5-11

95. 1 Corinthians 15:12-19

96. 1 Corinthians 15:20-58

97. 1 Corinthians 15:5-8

98. 1 Corinthians 15:5

99. Acts 1:15-26

100. For example, see Mark 9:31-32

101. Matthew 26-27; Mark 14-15; Luke 22-23; John 18-19

102. Luke 24:11

103. 1 John 1:1-4; Luke 24:36-43

104. Acts 1:21-22

105. Acts 1:4-11

106. Acts 2:36

107. Acts 3:8

108. Acts 3:11-13

109. Acts 3:14-15

110. Acts 4:18

111. Acts 4:20

112. 1 Corinthians 15:6a

113. 1 Corinthians 15:6b

114. 1 Corinthians 15:7

115. Warren W. Wiersbe, *The Bible Exposition Commentary*: NT, vol. 2, (Wheaton, IL: Victor Books, 1996), 335.
116. Matthew 10:1-4; Luke 6:12-16
117. Luke 6:16
118. Mark 6:3
119. Zechariah 9:10
120. Mark 3:20-21
121. John 7:5
122. James 1:1
123. Grant R. Osborne, "Introduction to James" in *ESV Study Bible* (Wheaton: Crossway, 2008), 2619.
124. 1 Corinthians 15:7
125. Acts 9:1
126. Acts 9:1-22
127. Kara Edie, "Lew Wallace: Atheist?"; accessed 10 April 2020: https://www.ben-hur.com/lew-wallace-atheist/.
128. Carol Wallace, "Ben-Hur: How Lew Wallace Found Faith in Epic Fiction," Guideposts, 26 July 2016; accessed 10 April 2020: https://www.guideposts.org/better-living/entertainment/books/ben-hur-how-lew-wallace-found-faith-in-epic-fiction.
129. Edie, "Atheist?"
130. Carol Wallace, "Ben-Hur."
131. Edie, "Atheist?"
132. Stephanie Cain, "Religious Conversion in Ben-

Hur"; accessed 10 April 2020: https://www.ben-hur.com/religious-conversion-in-ben-hur-lecture-video/.

133. "Josh's Bio," Josh McDowell Ministry; accessed 11 April 2020: https://www.josh.org/about-us/joshs-bio/.

134. Lee Strobel, *The Case for Christ: A Journalist's Personal Investigation of the Evidence for Jesus* (Grand Rapids: Zondervan, 1998).

135. "About Lee Strobel," Lee Strobel; accessed 12 April 2020: https://leestrobel.com/about.

136. John 5:24

137. At the end of our prayers "Amen" means, "So be it, Lord" (Jeremiah 11:5) "Lord, please do what I asked."

138. Zodhiates, *Word Study Dictionary*, s.v., ἀμήν, *amén.*

139. Isaiah 65:16

140. Titus 1:2

141. Romans 3:23

142. Zodhiates, *Word Study Dictionary*, s.v., ἁμαρτάνω, *hamartánō.*

143. Matthew 5:48

144. 1 Corinthians 15:3

145. Romans 3:10

146. Romans 6:23

147. Luke 16:19-31; Revelation 14:11

148. Romans 3:20

149. John 1:1, 14

150. John 3:16

151. 1 Peter 2:22, 24

152. Ephesians 2:8-9

153. D. James Kennedy, with a foreword by Billy Graham, *Evangelism Explosion*, 3rd ed. (Wheaton, IL: Tyndale House Publishers, 1983), 36.

154. Ephesians 2:8-9

155. Kennedy, *Evangelism Explosion*, 40.

156. John 3:5

157. James 1:18; 1 Peter 1:23-25

158. Warren W. Wiersbe, *The Bible Exposition Commentary: NT*, vol. 1 (Wheaton, IL: Victor Books, 1989), 295.

159. John 16:8

160. John 16:9

161. Romans 10:17

162. "Spiritual faith refers specifically to the act of trusting what God has said—revealed to man (Gen 2:17; Matt 8:8-10; John 3:1-3; Rom 3:22). Spiritual faith is a gift given by God in creation as are all the endowments of man. It is also a gift in the sense that God restores the ability to exercise spiritually-restorative faith as a sinner through the provision of grace enablements (John 12:35-36; Eph 2:8)." Ronnie W. Rogers, *Does God Love All or Some? Comparing Biblical Extensivism and Calvinism's Exclu-*

sivism, with a foreword by Adam Harwood (Eugene, OR: WIPF & Stock, 2019), 270.

163. Matthew 18:2-3

164. 1 Corinthians 15:4

165. John 5:23

166. Acts 16:31

167. John 10:30

168. 1 John 2:23

169. 1 John 1:7

170. John 6:37

171. John 1:12

172. "No condemnation," means "no sentence of judgment." Zodhiates, *Word Study Dictionary*, s.v., **κατάκριμα**, *katákrima*.

173. Romans 8:1

174. Job 1:6-12; 2:1-7

175. John 5:22

176. Romans 8:33-34

177. Ephesians 2:1-3

178. John 5:25

179. Colossians 1:13-14

180. Jeremiah 17:9

181. John 16:8-9

182. Romans 10:13

Mark H. Ballard, faithful pastor, diligent church planter, passionate evangelist, innovative educator, creative and prolific author, pacesetting Baptist leader, is the husband of Cindy and dad of Benjamin. He graduated Criswell College with his Bachelor's, and Southeastern Baptist Theological Seminary with his M.Div. and PhD. Dr. Ballard, a native of Colorado, serves as the founding president of Northeastern Baptist College in Bennington, Vermont, and as a member of the Conservative Baptist Network Steering Council. Prior to launching NEBC, he served as a church planter and pastor in New Hampshire, Virginia, Florida, North Carolina, and Texas. Mark has filled pulpits, held revival services, and served as a conference speaker in numerous states for more than 30 years.

Timothy K. Christian serves as Adjunct Professor of Theology at Northeastern Baptist College and as Senior Pastor at Stamford Baptist Church in Stamford. Connecticut. Prior to this assignment, Dr. Christian served as a professor and administrator at Mid-America Baptist Theological Seminary. Dr. Christian also served as a pastor, transitional pastor, conference speaker, contributing editor, and co-author of several works. Tim is married to his lifelong friend and partner Judy. They have two married children, and seven grandchildren.

Other Books by Mark H. Ballard and Timothy K. Christian

Open Doors: The Pathway to God-Sized Assignments is an exciting account of God's supernatural activity. God opens doors— mega doors. He works mightily in, and for, those who see His doors and walk through by faith. Using faithful biblical exposition and inspiring personal illustrations, *Open Doors* invites you to join what God alone can do.

Priorities: Reaching the life God Intended is written to help you discover and accomplish your God-given priorities. In its pages, you will learn a simple process drawn from Ballard's practical expositions of Haggai. This process will guide you to use rather than lose your time. *Priorities* will help you invest your talents and treasures wisely and effectively.

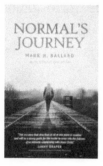

Normal's Journey is a fascinating and compelling description of one man's search for satisfaction and fulfilment. Through his search, he discovers that the dissatisfaction that overwhelmed his life is rooted in his lack of intimacy with his Lord Jesus Christ. His journey— *Normal's Journey*—is our own story, of seeking the full life found only in Christ.